To my parents and to their
"granddogs"—
The "Resounding" Poodles

"I WANT A PUPPY!"

Everyone loves puppies!
Puppies are playful and cuddly.
God knows all about the things
you want, like puppies, ice cream,
and candy.
God knows that some of what you
want is good for you and that some
of it isn't.

God loves you.

He wants you to be happy.

If you want a puppy, that's fine.

God understands.

He will help you and your parents
decide if you should have a puppy.

Puppies are lots of fun, but they are
lots of work, too.
A puppy isn't a toy.
You can't put it back on the shelf
when you're tired of playing with it.

God wants us to care for our animals.
When he created the world, he
told Adam and Eve to take care of
everything he made.
If you get a puppy, you need to help
care for him!

These things can help you know if you are ready for a puppy:

•**Ask God what is best for you.**
Sometimes we think we know what is best. We forget to ask God what *he* wants. The Bible reminds us to ask God before we do anything.
"If you want to know what God wants you to do, ask him. He will gladly tell you" (James 1:5).

•**Ask your parents how you can prove you are ready to have a puppy.** Doing your chores well and on time will show your parents they can count on you. God says we need to do little things well before we try bigger things. *"You have been faithful over this small amount. So now I will give you much more"* (Matthew 25:23).

**•Ask your friends who have dogs
to show you how they take care
of their pets.**
God tells us that our friends can help
us learn.
*"Don't go ahead with your plans
without the advice of others" (Proverbs
20:18).*

•**Decide what kind of puppy you want.** Do you want a puppy that grows up to be a big dog?

Or do you want a small dog that can curl up in your lap?

Do you want a fluffy, furry dog or a smooth, shiny dog?

Find out more about different dogs.

Read books or ask your parents to take you to a dog show.

"HI, LITTLE PUPPY! WELCOME HOME!"

God wants you to feel loved and safe.
He does special things to help you
feel that way.
He watches over you.
He gives you love letters in the Bible
and parents who love you.
He gives you food every day and a
safe, warm home.
God always loves and takes care of
you!

A new puppy needs to feel loved and safe, too.
Puppies show you love by licking your face, wagging their tails, or snuggling close to you.
The love between you and your puppy is special.

There is a special love between you
and God, too.
When things are new or scary, you
can trust God to keep you safe.
Your puppy will learn to trust you
when you take good care of him.
Your puppy will feel your love, just
like you feel God's love.
Do these things to help your new
puppy feel safe and loved:

•Give him his own name right away.

Pick just the right one. Don't change it.

Say your puppy's name whenever you talk to him.

The Bible says that God knows you by name, just like a shepherd knows each one of his sheep.

"A shepherd leads his sheep, calling each by its pet name" (Isaiah 40:26).

•Talk to him in a low, soft, happy voice. Don't make loud noises.

Don't let anyone tease your puppy. The Bible tells us that *"kind words are like honey. They are nice to hear and they bring health"* (Proverbs 16:24).

•Watch him when you play.
Don't let your puppy wander away or
get into trouble. Put away anything
that could hurt him. You need to keep
him safe, just like God keeps us safe!
*"You even keep me from getting into
trouble!" (Psalm 32:7).*

•**Hold him carefully.** Put one hand under your puppy's chest or around his shoulders. Put your other hand under your puppy's hind legs. If your puppy wiggles, don't grab too tight. Put your puppy down gently. Hold your puppy just like God holds you: gently and safely! You are so close to God. It's almost like he is right there beside you. *"You love me! You are holding my right hand!"* (Psalm 73:23).

YOUR PUPPY DEPENDS ON YOU!

The Bible tells us how great God is.
He knows how much we need him.
He never stops taking care of us.
Not even for a minute.
Psalm 23, a special song in the Bible,
tells us that God is our Shepherd. He
gives us food, water, and rest. He
keeps us safe from danger.

You need to be a "shepherd" for your puppy. He counts on you to meet his needs! When your puppy gets hungry, he can't open a bag of dog food. You have to care for him. Plan jobs so that everyone in your family has something special to do to take care of your puppy.

Your puppy needs these things every day:

•**Food for breakfast, lunch, and dinner.** Put your puppy's food in a clean dish. Give him his food at the same times in the same place every day. God gives us food every day, too! Be sure to tell him thank you. *"You give me good food" (Psalm 23:5).*

•Fresh, cold water in a clean dish.
Be sure your puppy can get to the
water dish, and that there always is
plenty of water. The Bible tells us that
God gives us good things to drink,
too. *"He leads me beside the quiet
streams" (Psalm 23:2)*.

•**Time to rest.** Give your puppy his own bed. A box with a clean towel or blanket inside is nice. God reminds us that girls and boys need time to rest and sleep, too! *"He lets me rest. . . . He gives me new strength" (Psalm 23:2-3).*

•**Time outside to play and to go potty.** Little puppies need to go outside about once an hour when they are awake.

Tell your puppy, "Good dog!" when he goes potty outside. If your puppy makes a mistake inside, don't get angry. Say, "Do you want to go out?" Then take your puppy outside to help him remember. We make mistakes, too. But God is patient and loving with us. He teaches us how to do what is right. *"You are close beside me . . . guarding and guiding all the way" (Psalm 23:4).*

WOW!
LOOK AT THAT
PUPPY GROW!

Everyone thinks babies are cute.

God loves us when we are babies.

He loves us when we are grown up.

And he loves us when we are in between!

God's love for us lasts forever!

People grow up fast. But puppies grow
up even faster. Sometimes when
puppies grow up, they don't
seem cute anymore.

But you need to love your growing dog
just as much as you did when he was
little. Remember, real love lasts
forever. Just like God's
love for us.

These things will help your dog grow up healthy:

•**Take him to the veterinarian (animal doctor) for checkups and shots.** God tells us in the Bible that good health is important.
"Dear friend . . . I pray that your body is as healthy as I know your soul is" (3 John 1:2).

•**Take him to the dog groomer for a bath and haircut.** The groomer will show you how to clean your dog's eyes and ears and how to keep his toenails short.

•Give him play times.
Growing dogs have lots of energy!
Give your puppy safe toys, like nylon
bones or hard rubber balls.
Don't let him chew the wrong things
like shoes, plants, or electrical cords.
Puppies like to chew a lot!
That's because when puppies are
around five months old, they lose
their baby teeth and get grown-up
teeth.

•Give him a nylon or leather collar that fits right as he grows. Your dog also needs a leash for walks (not a rope or chain). Be sure to get your puppy a dog license or tag that tells where he lives.

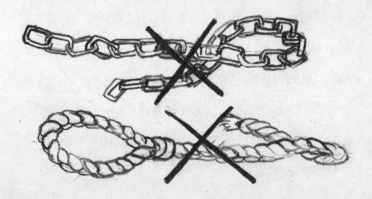

5

DOGS LOVE GAMES AND TRICKS!

We make God happy when we obey him. Obeying God makes us feel warm and happy, too. His rules are right and good. They help keep us safe. Sometimes we don't want to follow God's rules. We want to do things our own way instead of listening to God or to our parents. That makes God sad. But he will forgive us if we say we are sorry.

Growing puppies need to learn the
rules, too. They are happiest when
they obey you and make you happy.
You and your family make the rules
for your puppy. Some of those rules
could be "Don't jump on people" and
"Don't bite."

We learn God's rules by going to
church, reading the Bible, talking to
God in prayer, and obeying our
parents. Your puppy can learn your
rules by going to dog obedience school.
Your whole family can take your
puppy to dog school so you all will
know how to help your puppy obey.

Puppies love to learn tricks.
You can teach your puppy how to
sit up, shake hands (give you five),
dance, or fetch.
Puppies also love to run races with
you or catch Frisbees.

Remember these tips when you teach
your puppy:

•**When he does what you ask, praise
him.** Say, "You are such a good dog!"
Or, "That was just right!" Dogs like
praise. People like praise, too. When
you do something just right, it feels
good when someone praises you. The
Bible says praise is good.

*"Praise her for the many fine things she
does" (Proverbs 31:31).*

•**If he makes a mistake, tell him, "No."** Then show him what you want. Be calm and gentle when you train your dog. The Bible tells us that if we really love someone, we will be patient.
"Love is very patient and kind" *(1 Corinthians 13:4).*

•Give him treats or rewards when he obeys.

A good treat is a small piece of a hot dog, about the size of a penny.
(Don't give your dog too many treats. He could get an upset tummy.)
Giving your puppy rewards lets him know you are proud of him, that you like what he did.

God likes to let us know he is proud of us, too. He promises to reward us when we obey him.

"You reward everyone according to his life and deeds" (Jeremiah 32:19).

•Take ten minutes each day to teach him.

Teaching your puppy every day is the best way for him to learn and remember.

It is the best way for people to learn, too.

Ask God every day to help you do the right things.

"Keep me from doing wrong things. . . . I want my words and thoughts to please you" (Psalm 19:13-14).

CONCLUSION

God made you. Even before you were born, God loved you. The Psalms tell about God's great love for each of us: *"Thank you for making me so wonderfully! . . . You saw me before I was born. You planned each day of my life. . . . How great to know you think about me all the time"* (Psalm 139:14, 16-18).

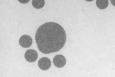

God loves you with a forever love. He wants you to know his Son, Jesus Christ. Jesus did something wonderful for you! He came to earth and died on a cross so that you could live forever with God. But Jesus didn't stay dead! He rose from the dead and is alive right now with God. Jesus wants you to believe in him so that you can live with him and God forever.

If you would like to know Jesus, tell
him right now! Tell him you need him.
Tell him you are sorry for the times
when you didn't do what he wanted.
Ask him to show you what he wants
you to do. Jesus loves you—he will
answer your prayer.

You can give something wonderful back to God by thanking him for his special care. God likes to hear our thanks. Even the animals thank and praise God! The Bible says to *"let the wild animals . . . praise him"* (Psalm 148:10).

God loves the animals he created.
When you take care of your puppy,
you are taking care of something
God loves very much.

Make God happy by loving and caring for your puppy.
And say thank you to God every day for giving you the wonderful gift of a special puppy to love!

A WORD TO PARENTS

Most children benefit from growing up with a pet. The animal-human bond teaches us about the human-divine bond. The unconditional love dogs lavish on humans can be a glimpse of God's unconditional love. The unwavering trust dogs bestow upon their owners is exemplary of the trust that we can show our Provider.

Meeting the responsibilities of puppy care gives children increasing self-esteem. Children can also gain a fairly realistic picture of the demands of parenting. The developmental stages from puppyhood to adulthood help children witness a "fast forward" of human maturation, including the realities of puberty (sexual development) and adolescent independence (potential problem behaviors). Assigned tasks and shared puppy-care duties teach children the importance of teamwork, meeting deadlines, coping with routines, and becoming someone dependable.

Consider these things as you decide whether or not to have a puppy.

Do *you* want a dog? Puppies need *adult* leaders to grow up physically and psychologically healthy. Studies show that most family dogs bond with the adult female in the household. Are you willing to sacrifice time, energy, and money? Are you ready for stains on your perfect carpet, tunnels in your backyard, mangled shoes, and the thousand other little "joys" puppies can bestow upon you along with that famous "unconditional devotion"? Don't buy a puppy just for your child! You have to live with the puppy as well.

Don't bring a puppy home "on trial," either. "Trial puppies" can sense the lack of security and usually end up being a trial! If you're not ready to bring a puppy into your household, don't! All of you—puppy included—will regret it. (You can work out compromises, though. For example, consider a "foster puppy program" where your child spends some time each week baby-sitting a friend's dog.)

Take time to find the right puppy. Learn about different breeds of dogs. Check *Simon and Schuster's Guide to Dogs* (Simon and Schuster, Inc.), or *The Perfect Puppy: How to Choose Your Dog by Its Behavior* by Hart and Hart (W.H. Freeman and Company). If possible, choose a purebred dog and *always* buy from a reputable breeder. Call kennel clubs in your area for additional information on breeds and breeders.

When choosing your puppy, use both "heart" and "head." The ideal family pet is one with a middle-of-the-road temperament: not too aggressive, but not a shrinking violet. Ask to see the puppy's mother (dam) and father (sire), if possible. Play with the entire litter of puppies. Do not allow the breeder to select one for you. Have your puppy examined by your vet within twenty-four hours of purchase. Have the seller sign a written agreement that the pup may be returned for full refund if the vet finds any problems.

Don't expect too much from your child. Don't overload a young child with pet-care responsibilities. Three- to five-year-olds need lots of supervision with puppy-care tasks. Five- to eight-year-olds can be responsible for basics (i.e., cleaning and refilling puppy's water bowl, helping prepare puppy's food at dinnertime). But even they will need reminders.

Realize that the novelty of a new puppy will wear off and your child may lose interest in the puppy and puppy chores. If this happens, try restoring interest with puppy kindergarten (early obedience training). Or post a check-off chart of puppy care tasks for each day of the week, rewarding completed tasks with a "seal of puppy approval"—a colorful dog stamp or sticker—at the end of the week.

	MON	TUES	WED.	THURS	FRI.	SAT.	SUN.
FEED	✓	✓					
WATER	✓	✓					
WALK	✓	✓					
BRUSH	✓						
BATH	✓						
TREATS?	✓	✓					

Share successes and keep encouraging! Praise your *child* each time the puppy does right. If there are struggles or failures, do not use the puppy as a "bargaining chip" with children. Don't threaten to give the dog away if children repeatedly forget their puppy chores or if puppy misbehaves. Giving a dog away shatters the companion bond and can damage a child's self-esteem. Children sometimes wonder if they, too, can be "given away" for not measuring up!

Keep your cool! Puppies can fill our lives with wonder and delight in God's creation. Growing dogs can fill our lives with faithful companionship. But sometimes you face problem puppy behaviors. Chewing, digging, soiling in the house, excessive barking are all typical adolescent dog behaviors. Don't hesitate to consult experts, especially if you are a first-time dog owner.

Some excellent books on puppy raising are *Mother Knows Best: The Natural Way to Train Your Dog,* by Carol Lea Benjamin (Howell Book House, Inc.) and *How to Be Your Dog's Best Friend,* by the Monks of New Skete (Little, Brown and Company). (These books contain wonderful tips for training kids and spouses, too, if you have a creative mind!) Also, talk to your puppy's breeder or to others who are experienced, especially with dogs of your puppy's breed. Call local kennel clubs to get in touch with helpful resource people.

If problems become severe, especially if biting or nipping are problems, consult a professional dog obedience trainer immediately! Most "problem" dogs are good dogs who don't understand the rules of doggy etiquette—usually because the rules haven't been clearly defined or consistently enforced by their owners. Even dogs with the most frustrating problem behaviors generally respond to professional help.

Help your child to see the wonder and goodness of God's creative love in the life of your little puppy!

Psalm 36:5-7 in *The Bible for Children* reads in part, "Your steadfast love, O Lord, is as great as all the heavens. . . . You are concerned for men and animals alike. How precious is your constant love, O God!" In his wisdom, God calls us to be masters of his creation. Jesus shows us that being a master doesn't mean dominance, but servant leadership, commitment despite disappointments, and delight in others' unique qualities.

A puppy's love is uncomplicated, joyous, and tail-wagging. What a wonderful gift to give your child! When you let your child have a puppy to love, you offer him or her an opportunity to witness the creativity, compassion, faithfulness, and delight that our Creator lavishes on all his creation. And you direct your child to the Giver of all good things: the one true God!

Ask your bookstore for other Eager Reader books:

Corey's Dad Drinks Too Much
Stranger Danger
Natalie Jean and the Flying Machine
Natalie Jean Goes Hog Wild
Natalie Jean and Tag-along Tessa
Natalie Jean and the Haints' Parade
Alfred MacDuff Is Afraid of War
Three Cheers for Big Ears
Harold's Dog Horace Is Scared of the Dark

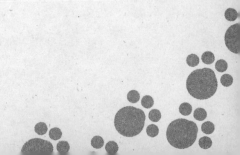